VALENTINES FOR ALL

Esther Howland Captures America's Heart

Nancy Churnin

illustrated by
Monika Róża Wiśniewska

Albert Whitman & Company
Chicago, Illinois

Even as a child, Esther Howland had a lot to say. Her family and friends often kept their feelings to themselves. But not Esther! If she loved someone, she let them know. Valentine's Day was her favorite holiday, and each year, she drew big hearts around her words.

Roses are red.
Lilies are white.
Making hearts
happy fills me
with delight.

Not many people in the 1800s celebrated Valentine's Day the way Esther did. In those days, most Americans thought the holiday was a waste of time. That's why in 1847, when Esther was nineteen years old, she was surprised by the present her father brought her from England.

She ran her fingers over the red paper heart trimmed with lace. She opened the pale green envelope on the center of the card, pulled out a poem, and... *whoa!* What was this wonderful thing? Esther could see in her father's eyes how much he hoped the card would let her know he loved her. It did! And that got her thinking...

Roses are red.
Violets are blue.
I've got an idea for something new.

"It will never take off," Esther's brothers said when she suggested selling handmade valentines. "People in England like fancy things. Americans don't." Esther's father and brothers ran the family's paper company, S. A. Howland & Sons. Women like Esther weren't expected to understand or work in business. But Esther's father encouraged her to explain her plan.

Roses are red.
Daffodils—yellow.
My cards speak
for you if you're
a shy fellow.

Esther said that many people—including her brothers!—had big feelings
they couldn't always express. Esther's cards could help put those feelings into
words. All she needed was colored paper and lace for her designs.

Roses are red.
Petunias are pink.
Cutting and gluing
helps me think.

Her father tallied the cost. Two hundred dollars? That was a lot! Still, Esther persisted. She promised to earn the money back. She got to work creating a dozen different valentines for one of her brothers to take on a sales trip.

As she waited for him to return, she worried. She had put her whole heart into her cards. Would people like them?

Finally, her brother came home. He handed her a piece of paper. Esther blinked and stared. Five *thousand* dollars' worth of orders? And people wanted them fast!

Her brother grinned. "I guess you'll need more paper and lace!"

Sitting at her desk, Esther imagined thousands of her valentines passing from hand to hand, connecting hearts. Then a thought shook her out of her dream: there was no way she could make all of the cards before Valentine's Day! Unless...

Roses are red.
Dahlias are lime.
How can I make so many in time?

Early in the morning, a team of Esther's friends clumped and creaked up
to the bedroom Esther had turned into an office. One woman cut. *Snip, snip!*
Another wrote. *Scritch, scratch!* Another pasted words, lace, and ribbon.
Smoosh!

With the help of her friends, Esther's business took off. Just as she had hoped, her valentines captured people's hearts. Still, she had more to say!

She brought sketches for new cards on her walks. She studied faces to see which words people stumbled over, which ones made their eyes glow or their smiles grow.

Roses are red.
Jasmine is beige.
My cards make
hope fly like birds
from a cage.

Finding the right words was important, but Esther knew that pictures and pretty decorations could speak to people in ways that even her best poems couldn't. She bought fancy ornaments to add sparkle to her cards. She added thin layers of gold called gilt. She even created flaps that lifted to reveal secret messages and compartments that held surprise gifts.

With each new design, Esther helped more and more people show they cared. In response, each year, more and more people went to shops looking for cards stamped with the letter *H*, for Howland.

Roses are red.
Shamrocks are green.
My cards are the heart-iest any have seen.

Then, in April 1861, the Civil War began. The Northern states were fighting the Southern states, which meant that sometimes families, friends, and sweethearts were divided. This sad, painful time didn't seem right for fancy cards or messages of love. But to Esther's surprise...

Roses are red.
Pussy willows are gray.
When people are hurting,
I know what to say.

In early February, a woman knocked on Esther's door, hoping to find a valentine to send her husband, who was off at war. "It will keep his courage up," the woman said. Her eyes were wet and thankful when Esther gave her the perfect card.

More knocks followed. Some people placed orders for entire companies of soldiers. On her walks, Esther saw women kissing valentines they'd received from soldier sweethearts. She had created her cards to celebrate love. Now she saw that cards could ease pain.

Roses are red.

Asters are teal.

Cards that share
love help hearts
to heal.

Esther began to wonder how her cards could help people share feelings throughout the year. She thought and thought, and soon she was creating birthday and holiday cards. Want to say you're sorry? Want to promise to be friends forever? Her cards could help with that too!

Roses are red.
Night tulips are black.
Looking for words?
They're in my card rack.

Then, in 1866, Esther slipped and injured her knee. Even with the help of doctors, she would never walk again. Still, Esther kept finding new ways to help others say what they were feeling. She printed a book of poems so people could cut and paste the words they wanted most—in red, green, blue, or gold ink—inside the cards they liked best.

Esther never married or had children. But she inspected each card like a proud parent making sure her child was impeccably dressed.

Roses are red.

Lilacs are plum.

When my cards bring joy, it makes my heart hum.

In 1880, Esther's world was changing. Her beloved father had fallen ill. Printing presses had made it easier and faster to create cards that cost less than Esther's handmade ones, making it hard for her to compete.

Roses are red.
Rhododendrons—cream.
I'm glad I had courage
to follow my dream.

Esther had poured her heart into helping people show they cared. She was proud of what she had accomplished. Now, it was time to retire and care for her father—and herself.

Still, every time she saw others exchange the fancy cards
she'd made popular…

she felt love fill her heart too.

Roses are red.
Forget-me-nots, blue.
Why don't you
make your dreams
come true?

Author's Note

Esther Howland, born August 17, 1828, in Worcester, Massachusetts, became an entrepreneur seven decades before women won the right to vote in 1920. It helped that her parents believed in her dream. Her father, Southworth Allen Howland (1800–1882), bought her supplies to start her business. Her mother, Esther Allen Howland (1801–1860), author of *The New England Economical Housekeeper and Family Receipt Book*, provided a model of a strong woman.

At a time when most women were discouraged from earning a living, Esther paid women to help her cut and paste in an assembly line, which she created before Henry Ford popularized the concept to build cars in the early twentieth century. If women were unable or uncomfortable with working outside their homes, she dropped off boxes of supplies with sample cards and picked up the boxes when they were done.

An astute businesswoman, Esther placed her first advertisement for her cards in the *Worcester Daily Spy* in February of 1850. She also protected her ideas. When others copied her designs, she stamped the letter *H* on the back of her cards in red ink along with the letters *N.E.V.Co.* for her business, the New England Valentine Company.

Esther charged five cents for simple cards and up to fifty dollars for fancy ones with hidden doors that hid locks of hair or engagement rings. After demand for valentines soared during the Civil War (1861–1865), Esther's business earned more than a hundred thousand dollars per year, the equivalent of about two million dollars today. While the family business was named S. A. Howland & Sons, it was the Howland daughter, Esther, who scored the greatest success.

In 1879, Esther merged her business with Edward Taft, the son of one of her competitors. Esther Howland and Edward Taft sold their company to George Whitney in 1880, when Esther retired to take care of her sick father, who had been living alone since Esther's mother died. Esther died March 15, 1904, at age seventy-five, in Quincy, Massachusetts.

You can see a tribute to Esther Howland at Worcester Historical Museum. I am grateful to Vanessa Bumpus, exhibits coordinator; Wendy Essery, library and archive manager; and everyone at the museum for help with this book.

Write Your Own Valentines

Poems have long been a popular way to express love, friendship, comfort, and cheer. The poems in this book are original poems based on still-familiar lyrics from *Gammer Gurton's Garland*, a British poetry collection compiled by Joseph Ritson of London: "The rose is red,/the violet's blue,/The honey's sweet,/and so are you."

One reason for using short, rhyming poems in your valentines is that like song lyrics, they are easy to remember. Many of the poems Esther wrote were made up of four short lines, with the last word of the second line rhyming with the last word of the fourth line. For example, a poem in one of Esther's cards reads: "In your heart/my home I view,/There I'll live/and love for you."

You can try other poetic forms, too, such as sonnets and limericks, each of which have a set number of lines grouped together to form stanzas, with each line having a certain number of syllables, or beats. You can write couplets (two-line stanzas), tercets (three-line stanzas), quatrains (four-line stanzas), cinquains (five-line stanzas), or sestets (six-line stanzas) or try haikus, acrostics, or free verse, which don't rhyme. Whatever and however you choose to write, if you share what is in your heart, your words, like Esther Howland's, will find a home in the hearts of others.

You can submit your valentines to the annual Worcester Historical Museum valentine card contest by visiting their website. If you send photos of your submissions to the contact page on nancychurnin.com, we'll be proud to showcase your cards there too.

Images from the collections at Worcester Historical Museum, Worcester Mass.

For my Valentines: my husband, Michael, and sons Ted, Sam, David, and Josh—NC

For Rui, who taught me that there is a significant difference between
"Te amo" and "Amo-te"—MW

Library of Congress Cataloging-in-Publication data is on file with the publisher.

Text copyright © 2023 by Nancy Churnin

Illustrations copyright © 2023 by Albert Whitman & Company

Illustrations by Monika Róża Wiśniewska

First published in the United States of America in 2023 by Albert Whitman & Company

ISBN 978-0-8075-6711-1 (hardcover)

ISBN 978-0-8075-6717-3 (ebook)

Printed in China

10 9 8 7 6 5 4 3 2 1 WKT 28 27 26 25 24 23

Design by Mary Freelove with the help of Erin McMahon

For more information about Albert Whitman & Company,
visit our website at www.albertwhitman.com.